# The Christmas That Didn't Need Wrapping

By Dandi Daley Mackall     Illustrated by Dawn Mathers

AUGSBURG • MINNEAPOLIS

THE CHRISTMAS GIFTS THAT DIDN'T NEED WRAPPING

Copyright © 1990 Augsburg Fortress

ISBN 0-8066-2466-3     LCCN 89-82553

Manufactured in the U.S.A.                                    AF 9-2466

94   93   92   91   90   1   2   3   4   5   6   7   8   9   10

*With love,*
*to Danny, my stepson*

"I *like* decorating our Christmas tree! I don't like wrapping presents. It's too hard. This is easy!" said Kay.

Kay's big brother, Jay, stood on the dining room chair and tried to place the tinsel, one piece at a time, over the longest branch of the pine tree.

"Well," said Jay, "wrapping presents isn't so hard once you get the hang of it."

Kay stopped throwing her tinsel at the tree and looked up at her brother. "I love Christmas!" she said.

Mom walked in just in time to see Kay aim her last piece of tinsel at the tree. "It's the most beautiful tree I've ever seen!" she declared. "You two have done a wonderful job decorating!"

Kay made a face that scrunched up her nose. "Mommy, do you really think it's the most beautiful tree ever?" she asked.

"Aw," Jay whispered to his little sister. "Mom says that every year."

Mom laughed. "I say our tree is more beautiful every year because it seems that way to me. Celebrating Jesus' birthday gets better and better each Christmas."

Jay heard the doorknob turn. "Dad's back with the mail!" he shouted.

"Daddy," Kay called, running up and grabbing his arm. "Come see our beautiful Christmas tree!"

"You guys aren't ready for Christmas to come, are you? We still have four more days!" laughed their father.

"I can't wait!" shouted Jay.

The next morning, Kay ran into Jay's room. She was still wearing her nightgown. "Get up, sleepy-head!" she called in a cheery voice as she tried to pull back the covers from Jay's head. "Is it Christmas yet, Jay?"

Jay sat up in bed, scratched his head, and tried to make his eyes stay open. Then he let out a big yawn. "Kay, it won't be Christmas for three more days," he said slowly. "And we've got plenty to do to get ready. Let's see. We've each got a present for Mom. And we got Dad a present when Mom took us to the mall."

"So what's left?" asked Kay.

Jay slid his feet into his bedroom slippers and pulled on his flannel robe. "Wrapping!" he said, bending over so he could look Kay straight in the eyes. "Today we wrap the presents."

Kay groaned. "But I don't like to wrap presents."

After breakfast, they cleared a spot on the floor in Jay's room so they could wrap presents. Mom got out the little pair of scissors for Jay, a roll of Scotch tape, and two long rolls of Christmas paper.

"I want this one," said Kay, as she grabbed for the red paper with green holly all over it.

"OK," Jay agreed. "I'll take the white and green paper."

Jay spread out the wrapping paper with green Christmas trees on it. Then he ran over to his closet and pulled down his secret sack. His baseball mitt, a Monopoly game, and a bag of leftover trick-or-treat candy fell from his top shelf. Jay kicked everything back into the closet and shut the door. With the sack behind his back, he yelled down the hallway, "Mom, don't come into my room. We're doing secret stuff!"

Jay handed Kay the little pencil holder she had made for Mom at Sunday school. Then he got out the book he was giving to Mom. Jay had made the book himself; he had drawn pictures on every page.

Finally, Jay pulled out the tie he and Kay had picked out for their dad. "Gosh, I hope Dad likes this tie," he said.

Kay took the tie from her brother and held it up. "He will. It's purple. I *like* purple."

"I know—it's your favorite color. I just hope it's Dad's too!" Jay said, laughing.

"Well," said Jay, "let's get busy!" Jay wrapped the book and the tie without much trouble.

Kay needed help tearing off the Scotch tape. And then she couldn't keep the paper taped together in the right places to cover her pencil holder. She needed more paper, then more tape.

"I give up!" cried Kay. "I can't make this pencil holder stay in the paper!"

Kay tried to push aside the piles of paper lying around her. "Jay," she began, "how come we have to wrap presents, anyway?"

"We just do." Jay was losing patience with his little sister. Why did she have to ask so many questions all the time?

"Well," Kay continued, "how many do we have to wrap?"

Jay started to say something about little sisters minding their own business, but he stopped himself. "Look, Kay. This is Christmas. We give lots of presents—to lots of people. It's not like a birthday, when only one person gets the presents."

All of a sudden Jay remembered something.

*Birthday!* he thought. *How could I forget?*

Jay jumped up and raced down the hall shouting, "Mom! Mom!"

Jay skidded to a stop outside Mom's den. He found her sitting at her desk. "Mom!" he said. "You gotta help."

"Jay," said his mother, "what's the matter? What is it?"

"Mom," Jay began, "I want to send Jesus a present for Christmas, but I don't know how to get it to him! And how could I ever wrap it?"

Mom stared at her son and then said gently, "I don't think it's possible to send Jesus a present, honey."

"But, Mom, in three days it will be Jesus' birthday. He gives us so many gifts, I want to give him a present—you know, to say thanks."

Mom motioned for Jay to sit down on the chair next to her desk. "Jay," she said, "you've come up with a wonderful thought. I'm glad you feel like giving to Jesus. But the best way to thank him for his gifts might be to give to other people—people you wouldn't think about otherwise."

"Oh, no!" Jay plopped his head down on the desk. "Does this mean more wrapping?"

"Not necessarily," said Mom. "Some of the best gifts that Jesus gives us don't come wrapped—like kindness, and love, and. . . ."

"I get it!" said Jay. "I'll come up with gifts for other people, gifts that don't need to be wrapped."

"That's it," Mom said. "Like patience and peace."

"And love!" exclaimed Jay.

Mom and Jay were interrupted by shouts from Jay's room. Kay sounded upset. "Jay! I can't get this stupid paper to do anything! Help me!"

"Sounds like a job for *patience*," said Jay, with a big smile.

"I think that sounds like a super way to thank Jesus," agreed Mom.

"Hang on, Kay!" shouted her brother, heading for the bedroom. "I'm on my way!"

The next day Jay woke up before Kay. *Two more days to Christmas*, thought Jay. *OK, Lord*, he prayed, *today I want to give one of those special no-wrap gifts to someone again—one every day until Christmas.*

Jay got his chance to give another "gift" that afternoon.

He and Max, his neighbor, built a giant snow fort in Jay's yard. Finally, they finished packing the last tower.

"OK," said Max, shoving Jay away from the front of the fortress. "I'm the king, and you're my slave."

"No way!" Jay yelled, pushing his way back to the front snow wall. "I'm king." Max always had to have things his way. Why didn't he stay in his own yard?

Max pushed Jay harder. Jay started to push him back. Then he remembered Jesus' birthday presents. *"Peace,"* he said under his breath.

"What did you say?" asked Max.

Jay looked at Max and stepped back. "Tell you what, Max. You can be king first. Then I'll take a turn at being king. Deal?"

Max stared at Jay. "What do you mean? Are you telling me you're going to let me be king, just like that?"

"Yep," Jay answered, smiling.

"I don't get it," said Max. "But you got yourself a deal, Jay. You're king next."

The boys played peacefully all afternoon.

That night it snowed. The next day, Jay and Kay couldn't wait to get outdoors and play.

"I love snow!" Kay told her brother, as she tried to make an angel in the deep, fresh snow.

But Jay was busy thinking. Finally, he spoke. "Kay, today I want to give *kindness*—you know, do something nice for someone. But I don't know what I can do. I can't think of anything."

"You can be kind to me if you want to," Kay offered.

"Thanks, Kay, but. . . ." Jay looked across the yard and saw Mrs. Cooper, dressed in a heavy black coat and a red scarf, trying to shovel the snow off her front sidewalk.

"That's it, Kay! Mrs. Cooper lives all by herself. She doesn't even have any kids. I can shovel her walks for her!"

"Me, too!" Kay shouted after her brother.

Kay wasn't much help shoveling, but Jay managed to scoop off all the sidewalks for Mrs. Cooper. Just as he finished with the last step, Jay saw his mother and sister walking toward him. Kay was carrying a tray of homemade Christmas cookies.

"We wanted to say Merry Christmas to Mrs. Cooper, too," said Mom.

Mrs. Cooper invited them all in for hot chocolate and cookies. Mom and Jay and Kay stayed and visited for a long time. Kay even recited the Christmas piece she learned for Sunday school. Mrs. Cooper seemed so much happier. "I'll never forget your kindness," she told them.

On Christmas morning, Mom brought out a special cake decorated with green letters that spelled MERRY CHRISTMAS. Mom, Dad, Jay, and Kay held hands around the table and sang, "Happy Birthday, Dear Jesus."

Then Dad prayed: "Father, thank you for the gift of your Son Jesus, the best gift of all! Amen."

"We have one more no-wrap present," Jay told Mom and Dad.

"Ready, Kay?" he whispered to his sister. "One . . . , two . . . , three. . . ."

"We *LOVE* you, Jesus!" Jay and Kay shouted as loud as they could. "MERRY CHRISTMAS!"